SAMURAI
STRATEGIES

Other Books by the Author
(Partial Listing)

SAMURAI
STRATEGIES

42 Martial Secrets from Musashi's
Book of Five Rings

Boyé Lafayette De Mente

TUTTLE PUBLISHING
Tokyo • Rutland, Vermont • Singapore

Published by Tuttle Publishing, an imprint of Periplus Editions (HK) Ltd,
with editorial offices at 364 Innovation Drive, North Clarendon, Vermont 05759
and 130 Joo Seng Road, #06-01/03, Singapore 368357.

ISBN 0-8048-3683-3
Printed in Singapore

Distributed by:

North America, Latin America & Europe
Tuttle Publishing
364 Innovation Drive
North Clarendon, VT 05759-9436
Tel: (802) 773 8930
Fax: (802) 773 6993
Email: info@tuttlepublishing.com
www.tuttlepublishing.com

Japan
Tuttle Publishing
Yaekari Building, 3rd Floor
5-4-12 Osaki, Shinagawa-ku
Tokyo 141-0032
Tel: (03) 5437 0171
Fax: (03) 5437 0755
Email: tuttle-sales@gol.com

Asia Pacific
Berkeley Books Pte. Ltd.
130 Joo Seng Road,
#06-01/03, Singapore 368357
Tel: (65) 6280 1330
Fax: (65) 6280 6290
Email: inquiries@periplus.com.sg
www.periplus.com

09 08 07 06 05
6 5 4 3 2 1

TUTTLE PUBLISHING® is a registered trademark of Tuttle Publishing

The way of the samurai is found in death. When it comes to either/or, there is only the quick choice of death. It is not particularly difficult.

— Yamamoto Tsunetomo in
Hagakure: The Book of the Samurai

ACKNOWLEDGMENT

I am indebted to my publisher Eric Oey for suggesting this book, and to my editor Ed Walters for making the text far more readable and useful to anyone wanting to achieve success in today's world.

Contents

Musashi's Book
of Five Rings

In 1974 Overlook Press, a small upstate New York publisher, brought out an English-language translation of
Miyamoto Musashi's *Go Rin Sho* (*Book of Five Rings*), a
small, esoteric treatise the famed samurai swordsman wrote
for his disciples just before he died in 1645. Soon afterward,
a columnist for *Advertising Age* mentioned it in a couple of
sentences, hinting that the fighting strategy and swords-

manship tactics it referred to were responsible for the astounding success of Japanese businessmen worldwide. This off-handed comment resulted in the book becoming an instant bestseller in two or three leading New York City bookshops. This got it reviewed by top magazines and newspapers nationwide, and before one could say *Nan Daro* ("What's going on?") it made the bestseller lists and stayed there for many months.

It is doubtful that very many of those who bought and read the small guide got much out of it. It was written for samurai warriors who were steeped in Buddhist and Shinto precepts, in the code of the samurai, in the long traditions of the samurai, and in allusions that were a part of the culture of the times. And like Japanese artists who leave it up to viewers to "complete" their work, Musashi left it up to readers of *Go Rin Sho* (Goh Reen Shoh) to fill in the details of his allusions and advice from their own store of knowledge.

The title of Musashi's treatise requires some explanation. It relates to the Buddhist concept of the so-called five elements: Earth, Water, Fire, Wind, and Void. In his view, the Earth represented the foundation of all things; Water represented the purity and fluidity of his style of fighting; Fire represented battle with its energy and ability to change direction; Wind represented other styles of fighting; and Void represented the place that all things come from. The Five-Element concept is widely used in Buddhist literature and teachings, and among other things is symbolized by the five-tiered pagoda that is so prominent in the Buddhist sphere of Asia.

In this book, I have attempted to identify and explain, in plain English, the philosophy, the strategy, and the "ways of winning" that Musashi sought to pass on to his disciples. His book is about how to fight duels to the death and win. The principles he introduces are equally applicable to winning in business, in sports, in war, and in virtually all other endeavors. I hope it helps you prevail over whatever challenges you may encounter.

— Boyé Lafayette De Mente

The Life and Times of Japan's Most Famous Samurai

The Samurai Era in Japan

During Japan's illustrious Heian Period, from 794 to 1185, the country was divided into provinces administered by governors sent out from the imperial capital of Heiankyo (present-day Kyoto). Most of these governors were excess imperial princes who had their own retinues of armed guards known as samurai, which means "one who serves" or "those who serve."

As the generations passed these provincial governors became more and more independent, gradually expanding the number of samurai they maintained and establishing their family clans as hereditary rulers of the provinces. During the same period, their samurai guards and armies evolved into a class of professional warriors that also became hereditary.

In the twelfth century leaders of the larger and richer provinces began to vie among themselves for hegemony. In the 1170s the Minamoto family clan began a military campaign to usurp the power of the Taira family, which had cemented its relationship with the imperial court by marrying sons and daughters into the imperial family, making them the virtual rulers of the country.

At a great sea battle off Dannoura in 1185 the Minamoto clan and their allies defeated the Taira forces. Those members of the Taira family not killed in battle drowned themselves— a tale recounted in the great novel *Heike Monogatari*, written by a court noble in the following century.

Minamoto clan leader Yoritomo, who had established his military headquarters in Kamakura, a tiny fishing village about an hour's train ride south of present-day Tokyo, consolidated his grip on the country, and in 1192 he forced the powerless emperor to officially designate him shogun, which is commonly translated as "generalissimo," in the sense of military dictator.

Yoritomo turned Kamakura into the administrative capital of Japan and proceeded to establish a feudal system that was to prevail in the country until 1868. He rewarded his allies by transforming the provinces they had ruled as governors into feudal fiefs and confirming them as their hereditary lords. Eventually these feudal lords came to be known as *daimyo* (die-m'yoh), or "great names."

The subsequent shoguns, fief lords and their samurai warriors became one of the most extraordinary classes of people ever to appear in any society, and they went on to rule Japan for the next 676 years. As time passed, all members of this ruling class, from the shogun down to the lowest warrior, came to be called samurai in a generic sense.

By the 1400s, the samurai class made up some 10 percent of Japan's population. With no wars to fight, the samurai had begun adding cultural achievements to their skills, combining rigorous daily practice in martial arts with studying the Chinese classics, poetry, calligraphy, painting, and pottery-making. The higher ranking the samurai, including the shogun, the more important learning became.

Peace generally prevailed until 1467, by which time the shogunate government had weakened and leading fief lords once again began to joust for supreme power. The next 101 years came to be known as the Sengoku Period (Warring States Period), which saw a series of skirmishes and battles between the more powerful *daimyo*.

Achieving extraordinary skill with the sword and other weapons became especially urgent for the samurai of this period. The shogunate and every fief and clan lord in the country had training *dojo* (doh-joh), "schools," staffed by master swordsmen. Dozens of fighting styles, some of them dating back several hundred years, were taught by these masters. Many new styles were also introduced.

During this period, samurai-turned-scholars began to record the ideal traits of the samurai, eventually producing a loose code of ethics that came to be known as *Bushido* (Buu-she-doe), or "The Way of the Warrior"—a code that was to mold the character and behavior of the Japanese in a way and to a degree never seen before, or since, in any society.

By the 1500s this code controlled every aspect of the lives of the samurai. The primary directives of the code required that they develop extraordinary skill with the sword and other weapons, dress and behave in a certain way, and be prepared to meet death at a moment's notice in the service of their lord—as well as to commit suicide and/or kill their families when that served the needs or wishes of their lords.

Just as present-day members of military forces are supported by the governments they serve, samurai who were formally recognized as members of the shogun's forces or the forces of fief lords received an annual stipend as their keep. They were forbidden to engage in ordinary work or commercial activity.

When this lord/retainer relationship was severed as a result of a fief being captured by some other *daimyo* or confiscated by the shogunate, the then masterless samurai became known as *ronin* (roh-neen), or "wave men," because they roamed the country, looking for work as bodyguards, freelance fighters, enforcers for unscrupulous samurai officials, spies, and so on.

By the last decades of the 1500s there were several hundred thousand displaced samurai roaming the country. In the larger battles of the time as many as 100,000 of them joined the forces of one fief lord or another.

The reputation of the *ronin* varied. Some remained upright and honest, scrupulously obeying the traditional samurai code of ethics. Others became ruthless rogues.

Another smaller group of independent samurai roamed Japan's great walking roads for a totally different purpose. These warriors were known as *shugyosha* (shuu-g'yoh-shah), which translates as "swordsman in training."

The *shugyosha* traveled the country seeking worthy opponents to meet in duels to hone their fighting skills. These duels were typically to the death, so they were not undertaken casually. Matches were sometimes arranged between individual *shugyosha*, and other times through fief lords and martial arts training schools.

The government recognized and condoned these duels as long as the participants followed the shogunate laws and customs. Some of the duels were impromptu meetings. Others were formally arranged, with notices sent out, and witnesses on hand. The reputation of *shugyosha* who had won many duels spread throughout the country, resulting in other "swordsmen in training" challenging them to fight.

Some *shugyosha*, like other *ronin*, also offered their services to warlords engaged in battles with each other. The aim of these "samurai in training" was to improve their skills and enhance their reputations by killing large numbers of warriors in single battles. This practice was known as "borrowing the battlefield."

Shugyosha who survived many duels and whatever battles they joined in generally ended up as masters, teaching the techniques that had made them successful.

Japan's Most Famous Samurai

The most remarkable and most famous of Japan's samurai was the legendary Miyamoto Musashi, who was born in 1584 and died of natural causes on May 19, 1645, at the age of sixty-one. The Japanese regard him as the epitome of the most admirable traits they have preserved from their samurai heritage—their ability to focus on specific goals, their continuing efforts to improve, their dedication to quality, their diligence, their perseverance, and their unquenchable spirit.

Perhaps the most incredible thing about Miyamoto Musashi is that he himself had no mentor or teacher—or so he claims, despite the fact that his father, Munisai, was a well-known swordsman who had mastered a number of fighting styles, was an instructor for the samurai of the powerful Shinmen clan, and once received a certificate from the reigning shogun naming him the leading swordsman of his time.

There is no record of Musashi having been trained by his father or anyone else, and it would appear that like prodigies in music, math, and other fields, he was born with a singular capacity that was to make him undefeatable in hand-to-hand combat.

It is, however, a matter of record that Musashi was one of those rare individuals able to grasp and absorb the essence of everything he observed and make it is own. It is also known that he met and exchanged insights with some of the most learned and skilled men of his day.

Musashi's relationship with his father remains something of a mystery. William Scott Wilson in *The Lone Samurai*, his wonderful biography of Musashi, recounts a tale told in *Tanji*

Hokin Hikki, another record of the times, that relates how from a very young age Musashi was a keen observer of the martial arts style of his father, Munisai.

But as the tale goes, the very young Musashi once had the temerity to criticize his father's use of the *jitte* (jeet-tay), a small metal rod that samurai used to deflect the blow of a sword. Munisai became so incensed at the criticism that he threw a carving knife at his son. Musashi dodged the knife, whereupon his father drew his short sword and threw it at him, apparently intending to wound him seriously, if not kill him. Musashi dodged the sword as well, and then ran away from home, going to his mother's village, where he lived with a priest who was related to his mother. The tale adds that Musashi never again returned to the home of his father, beginning his life as a loner and his rise to fame as the most formidable swordsman ever produced by the Way of the Samurai.

Big for a Japanese of that time and powerfully built—especially as a youth—Musashi was obviously endowed from childhood with abilities that made him one of the most extraordinary individuals in the history of Japan—a standout in a culture that produced great numbers of men who were master swordsmen as well as great scholars and superb administrators.

In his efforts to hone his fighting skills by engaging well-known swordsmen in combat, Musashi was an inveterate traveler, spending much of his life on the road, walking the great pedestrian highways that connected the country's two-hundred-plus fiefs with the shogunate capital, first in Kamakura, then in Yedo (Tokyo) and the imperial capital in Kyoto.

Musashi scorned accumulating material things, and throughout his life he journeyed from place to place with only the clothes on his back and his swords—often without money. Like an itinerant priest he depended upon the largess of others—fief lords, officials, and martial arts *dojo*—for room and board in exchange for lessons in his unique way of fighting. In between these occasions, and when on the road, he slept out in the open.

By today's standards, the physical hardships that Musashi endured during his travels were enough to try the soul of a saint. At least 70 percent of the time Japan is too hot or too humid, too wet or too cold. The annual spring rains last for weeks. Typhoons lash the islands in the late summer and fall. In winter, the mountains of the central and northern islands are covered in deep snow. But Musashi exposed himself to these conditions throughout his life as part of his physical and mental training.

Because of his obsession with mastering swordsmanship, Musashi never married, was apparently celibate much of his life, and admonished his disciples to avoid love entanglements and beware of women. Yet there is evidence that, like most men, he visited the courtesan quarters that were an integral part of Japanese society, and he is known to have formed an intimate relationship with one noted courtesan.

Musashi fought his first duel when he was thirteen years old, killing an exceptionally skilled *shugyosha* named Kihei Arima. According to Wilson, Arima was traveling about the country challenging all comers to fight in duels to the death. When he arrived in the village where Musashi lived, he set up a public sign, in gold letters, challenging anyone in the area to fight him. The young Musashi came across the sign and defaced it, writing that he accepted the challenge and would be there the following day.

When Arima was told that the challenger was a thirteen-year-old, he was incensed, but agreed to spare the boy's life if he would make a formal apology. The next day, Musashi showed up carrying a long wooden staff and accompanied by the priest he was living with, who apparently was acting as a go-between.

Instead of apologizing, Musashi rushed at the warrior with the wooden staff. The veteran samurai dodged the blow and drew his sword. After trying to strike Arima on the head, Musashi dropped his staff, rushed in, picked Arima up in the air, and threw him to the ground head first. Then he retrieved his staff, and crushed Arima's skull with two powerful blows.

Musashi fought his second duel in the spring of 1599, while on the road in a neighboring province. This time his opponent was a warrior named Akiyama, who is only identified as being "strong." Musashi was sixteen at this time. The following year he fought against the Tokugawa clan in the famous battle of Sekigahara, which led to the supremacy of Ieyasu Tokugawa and the founding of the famous Tokugawa Shogunate in 1603.

It is said that Musashi may have hoped that by demonstrating his extraordinary swordsmanship in a major battle he would be taken in as an instructor by one of the lords fighting against Tokugawa. But, despite his personal success in the battle, which was described as having made him famous among the warriors on both sides, the lord he chose to fight for was defeated. In any event, he continued to roam the country as a *shugyosha*, fighting in duels with noted swordsmen much like the later mythical gunslingers of the American West.

In 1604, when he was twenty-one, Musashi engaged and killed all of the leading swordsmen of the famous Yoshioka clan in Kyoto. In the first arranged encounter he killed the leader of the group. In the second encounter he killed the leader's brother. In the third encounter, at which all of the remaining members of the group were on hand, he killed the son of the leader and was immediately attacked by the entire group, over one hundred men. Undaunted, Musashi rushed into this army of warriors and in moments killed so many of them that the rest fled. This incredible feat made him a legend throughout Japan.

There were dozens of other samurai who were celebrated during their lifetimes as master swordsmen, at least one of whom is recorded as having killed some two hundred men in death duels. Many of these men wore flamboyant apparel. Some wore sashes declaring their pedigree and titles.

One of these men, Kojiro Sasaki, known as The Demon of the Western Provinces, was the sword instructor for the famous Lord Hosokawa and his samurai retainers. Musashi killed him in 1612 in what was to become his most famous duel.

Musashi wrote that he was able to defeat The Demon of the Western Provinces because he gave no thought to his own life; he simply walked in and struck. But Musashi was a breed apart from his famous contemporaries. He was a loner who dressed in simple clothing, never bragged, and often met his opponents in secluded places rather than in public. By the time he was twenty-nine, Musashi had met and killed more than sixty individual opponents. He then changed his lifestyle, becoming a master painter, calligrapher, poet, garden designer, and sculptor. He continued to roam the country, engaging in many duels with other samurai, some of them known throughout the land as masters of the sword.

But he had stopped killing all of his opponents. He merely prevented them from killing him, defending himself until they became exhausted and gave up, or until they recognized that they could not defeat him and stopped fighting. This often happened after they had made only a few attempts to cut him down, recognizing there was no way they could penetrate his defensive tactics.

In 1637, when he was already in his late fifties, Musashi fought for the Tokugawa Shogunate in the infamous Shimabara Rebellion, during which thousands of Japanese Christians and their *ronin* allies were slaughtered. The shogunate generals employed him as a consultant in besieging the rebels who had holed up in a castle.

In 1640, some four years before he retired and wrote *Go Rin Sho*, Musashi was asked by Tadatoshi Hosokawa, lord of the Hosokawa fief in Kumamoto, to write down the essence of his fighting style. In February of the following year, Musashi presented Hosokawa with a fifteen-page manuscript entitled *The Thirty-Five Articles of the Martial Arts*, which actually contained *thirty-six* articles. This manuscript became the outline for *The Book of Five Rings*.

In 1643, two years before his death (apparently from thoracic cancer), Musashi began living in the now famous Reigan Cave outside of Kumamoto City. Having developed such skill that he could not be defeated, Musashi began to reflect on the art of sword fighting and on winning. One of his rules was that the only goal in a fight was to win, and to win absolutely. This was the foundation of his philosophy, and it became the core of *Go Rin Sho*, in which he set down the principles of his winning techniques.

In April of 1645 Musashi retreated again to the cave where he had gone in the past to meditate and write, intending to die there. But his disciples carried him back to the house he had been living in as a guest of the local lord. He died the following month.

The Legend of Miyamoto Musashi

Soon after Musashi's death he became a favorite subject of Japan's large number of *kodan* (koh-dahn), or professional storytellers. Then, puppet and kabuki playwrights began creating dramas based on incidents in his life. Books about his exploits appeared shortly afterward.

The first movie based on Musashi's life appeared in 1908. Since then there have been more than forty other Musashi movies, one of the most popular of them starring the great actor Toshiro Mifune of *Seven Samurai* and *Yojimbo* fame.

The first English-language book on Musashi was written in the 1890s. Several more books about him, in both

Japanese and English, were written in the twentieth century. The most famous of these books, entitled *Miyamoto Musashi*, was started in 1935 by the great novelist Eiji Yoshikawa and serialized in the Asahi newspaper over the next four years.

Yoshikawa's book is based on the known facts of Musashi's life, built around a historically accurate framework of his times—the lifestyle of the common people, the way of life of the samurai and ronin, the rise of the Tokugawa Shogunate, the battles and intrigues of the fief lords, the introduction of Christianity and guns into the country, and finally the closing of the country to the outside world in 1635.

A significantly condensed version of Yoshikawa's huge book is available in an English edition entitled *Musashi*. Translated by Charles S. Terry, well known for his many masterful translations of Japanese literature, it is a perennial bestseller.

These books and movies made Musashi known to every Japanese and regarded as epitomizing many of the most admirable samurai-derived traits of the Japanese—their ability to focus on specific goals, their continuing efforts to improve, their dedication to quality, their diligence, their perseverance, and their unquenchable spirit.

Like the "art of war" manuals written by Sun Tzu, the fabled military master of ancient China, Musashi's strategies and tactics are based on deep insights into human nature combined with an uncommon level of pragmatism. His precepts about fighting and succeeding in any endeavor provide valuable lessons for anyone facing challenging circumstances—from the military and business to athletes and the "warriors" of everyday life.

The samurai culture, created over a period of nearly seven hundred years by Japan's ruling class of warriors and epitomized in *The Book of Five Rings*, still influences every facet of the Japanese way of thinking and doing things. Many Japanese, consciously and unconsciously, pattern their attitudes and behavior on the thinking and behavior of Musashi, including sacrificing themselves to ideals, and continuously striving to achieve perfection.

CHAPTER 1

Set Goals

In his *Book of Five Rings* Miyamoto Musashi makes two obvious points about goals: First, you must choose a goal before you can achieve it, and second, the more difficult and dangerous your goal is, the more effort you must put into achieving it.

Musashi's goal, which he established well before he reached his teens, was to become the best swordsman in his world. This would have been an ambitious goal at any time, but it was especially so in a world where swordsmanship was a matter of life and death for the class that ruled the country.

Musashi set out to be the best in a world that was already populated by many champion swordfighters who were obviously accomplished in the martial arts—demonstrated by the fact that they were still alive!

There are few, if any, goals in modern life that compare with the ones Musashi set for himself. But all achievement starts with goals, and Musashi emphasized that you should be ambitious in setting them. Ambitious goals will help you focus your energies, abilities, and actions to maximum effect.

CHAPTER 2

Life-or-Death Discipline

Only incredible mental, physical, intellectual, and spiritual self-discipline can explain how Musashi was able to become the finest swordsman in the country while still in his teens. Although records of Musashi's childhood are scarce, it is obvious that he was strong-willed and extraordinarily self-disciplined from an early age.

In his *Book of Five Rings* Musashi wrote that he had no teacher, that he was entirely self-taught. His claim is creditable: If one of the proud master teachers in the institutionalized and ritualized training system of the samurai, which kept careful records, could have claimed him as a student, they surely would have.

It is obvious that by the time he was thirteen he was extremely accomplished, at least with a wooden staff, so much so that he had no qualms about challenging a seasoned warrior who had killed many men in one-on-one combat.

This is enough to make Musashi unique in the annals of the samurai, and rare in any setting. It suggests that, as he claims, his ambition formed very early and drove him to a level of self-discipline that seems incredible for a young boy on his own.

Perhaps the best way to illustrate the degree of self-discipline required would be to compare it with what young men and women training for the Olympics would go through if they tried to become champions without the support of coaches, national associations, or sponsors.

There is, of course, nothing new about the role of discipline in developing skills of any kind. But Musashi's accomplishments make it crystal clear that achieving incredible results requires incredible discipline—knowledge that can be applied in any endeavor.

CHAPTER 3

Train to Win

The fighting skills that Miyamoto Musashi and other samurai developed, like those of Olympic champions, did not come easily. Although Musashi claimed to have been self-trained, we can assume that he based his training on the models provided by the most accomplished samurai instructors of the day.

Their programs were based on a regime of training that began in early childhood; was engaged in for several hours a day, generally six days a week; and continued for many years.

The formal training began when boys reached the age of six or seven. Around the age of fifteen, at which time they became full-fledge warriors, one of the common rites of passage was beheading several men who were either condemned convicts or captured enemies—to get the "feel" of cutting off a head.

Once the samurai had mastered the different weapons in their arsenal, particularly the sword, their training was reduced to a few hours a day several times a week—and continued until they died or retired.

Even samurai who became full-time administrators continued to practice with the sword. Those of higher rank, including shoguns, retained masters to teach them and serve as sparring partners.

For *shugyosha* like Musashi, intense daily training continued throughout their active lives because their lives depended upon their skills. They did not train just to engage in tournaments for show. They trained to uphold their honor and reputations and to stay alive.

To succeed in today's world, you too must keep yourself in "fighting trim" through constant and continuing training. Like the samurai, you need both physical and psychological exercises to stay physically sharp and mentally alert. You also need to continue training in your "weapons"—the special skills and techniques required by your field of endeavor—to survive and prosper.

CHAPTER 4

Be Prepared

Musashi endlessly repeated that knowing yourself, knowing your weapons, knowing your surroundings and your enemy or competitor are all as important as your skill in fighting or in negotiating. He was a master at preparing for a battle beforehand because his goal was to never leave anything to chance.

He taught that the warrior with the prepared mind is favored, no matter what weapon is used. On a number of occasions he fought skilled swordsmen in death matches using just a piece of wood to demonstrate this principle. The fact that he was victorious against so many opponents says volumes about his preparation and points out the importance of being prepared.

Musashi prepared himself meticulously not only for situations that he expected, but also for unexpected turns of events, so that only his opponents would be surprised. It is easy to understand how important this is if, like Musashi, you risk your life with every fight. But it is just as important if you expect to be successful in any field that requires quick decisions and split-second actions.

The principle of advance preparation is obviously known to both business and military people in the West. But even though they know it is vital to their chances of success, it is clear that a significant percentage of them do not put it into practice.

It goes without saying that spending time meticulously preparing for meetings, competitions, or other important events will give you an invaluable advantage against less-prepared opponents. And the more prepared you are—for the unexpected as well as the expected—the more successful you will be.

CHAPTER 5

The Illusion of Form

In the introduction to his way of fighting, Musashi departs completely from the prevailing attitudes about the martial arts and the way they were practiced at that time. He dismisses the traditional attachment to form and styles, saying they are like concentrating on the blossoms of a fruit tree and ignoring the fruit. This would seem to substantiate his claim that, unlike other young male members of the warrior class, he had no teachers and followed no established style.

Musashi as much as accused many martial arts instructors of the day—particularly Buddhist priests who claimed that their way of fighting was given to them by the gods—of being frauds. He went on to say that the traditional martial arts forms that had been taught for centuries had become barriers that prevented martial artists from being able to see the realities of engaging another person in a swordfight, especially when it was a duel to the death.

Apparently because his way of looking at swordsmanship and his method of fighting were so unorthodox, he did not try to explain them until he was on his deathbed. His way of teaching was to demonstrate his method of fighting in training sessions and demonstrations, leaving it up to his opponents, students, and onlookers to learn from the experience and from viewing him in action.

There were many stories during his early life that he himself was a fraud and that the victories he had won up to that time were flukes of one kind or another. On many occasions he was invited by fief lords and shogunate officials to engage them or one of their champions in demonstration bouts in the belief that he would be exposed as some kind of charlatan.

In over fifty years of dueling, fighting in wars, and demonstrating his techniques, beginning when he was only thirteen years old, Musashi never lost a single match. It is recorded that on one occasion the sword of an opponent cut a rent in the garment he was wearing—and that was the closest he ever got to suffering bodily harm.

The message that he taught over and over again, and in myriad ways, was that unfailing success in fighting and in any other endeavor is based on not being blinded by illusions—by grasping the essence of one's self, one's opponents or competitors, the task at hand, the circumstances of the physical location, and the surrounding environment. There is, of course, no better advice.

Despite his claim that he took nothing from the Buddhist scripts or any of the other teachings of the day, Musashi's outlook on life was pure Zen, which teaches how to recognize and deal with reality in a detached, objective way—minus the emotions that make life such a trial for so many people.

CHAPTER 6

Absolute Integrity

In his book *Bushido: The Soul of Japan*, Inazo Nitobe writes that the foundation of the code of samurai is justice—that nothing is more loathsome to a samurai than underhanded dealings and unjust behavior. He adds that the concept of justice is the power of deciding on a course of action in accordance with reason, without wavering, and in the words of a samurai, "to strike when it is right to strike and to die when it is right to die."

The level of integrity achieved in Japan during the reign of the samurai was unparalleled in history. The rules of the shogunate and the fief lords were clear and explicit. You followed the ethical standards that were the law of the land or you were punished, generally by a quick and often painful death.

Much of the morality that was prescribed during the samurai era regulated public behavior and was therefore visible for all to see. Morality was not based on religious precepts but on strict secular tenets designed to create a specific kind of harmony in Japanese society. This secular-based morality, now generally referred as "Japanese etiquette," was enforced by law, by custom, and by the acute sense of shame the Japanese felt when they failed to live up to these social standards.

By some measures, the traditional morality of the Japanese people has been significantly diluted since the introduction of democracy and individuality into the country after World War II. But by international standards, the Japanese as a whole are probably still the most moral people in the world.

How does such a strict standard of morality or integrity promote success? As in Musashi's time, adherence to moral and societal standards leaves no question as to the right way to act. With no ambiguity or uncertainty about behavior, competitors and combatants can focus on the task at hand. Along with other positive traits of the samurai character— discipline, honesty, loyalty, and perseverance—absolute integrity is critical to achieving success while upholding the standards of a moral society.

CHAPTER 7

Train the Mind

Musashi's main strength, as he said many times, was not in superior ability with weapons, but in using his mind to defeat his opponents. And it is obvious that at a very early age he trained his mind as vigorously as he did his body.

Except for the automatic functions of the body, the mind is the "software" that directs physical actions. Something causes the mind to "push a key" and the body reacts in a certain way. But this software is not built into the higher, civilized levels of the brain. It has to be "uploaded" through mental and physical training, preferably from early childhood.

Once this software has been "wired" into the brain it is not easy to change or erase, but it can be altered by additional, ongoing training. In other words, training the body can change the software that runs the brain, altering the way we think and act.

Early in their history the Japanese recognized and understood these fundamental principles of psychology and physiology, and they created a system of customs and rituals that were specifically designed to train both the mind and the body. In some of these practices, including the skills developed by the samurai, the physical training generally started before the individual was mature enough—intellectually, emotionally, and spiritually—to make a commitment to such an intensive program.

That is where the system of masters, mentors, and teachers—or in Musashi's case, extreme self-discipline—came in.

Both the physical and mental training of samurai youth began around the age of six or seven. The art of the sword and other weapons was studied and practiced daily for several hours.

By the time samurai youth were seven or eight years old it was as important to program their minds as it was to temper their bodies, if not more so. Their mental "software" had to be changed to provide the discipline necessary to achieve the goals of the training.

Young samurai boys were psychologically and philosophically programmed to be diligent, responsible, and fearless, and to look upon death as no more than a transition to another level of existence. They were trained to believe that death was preferable to failure and shame. Part of their training was to go to the execution grounds and practice cutting the heads and limbs off of criminals who had just been executed. More dedicated fathers and trainers provided the trainees with live criminals to behead.

At the age of fifteen they became full-fledged warriors and were required by the code of the samurai to wear two swords at all times when they were in public—a long sword, for fighting and enforcing the law, and a short sword to be used to commit *harakiri* (hah-rah-kee-ree)—that is, to kill themselves by slicing their stomach open—a custom that was so common that finally in the early 1600s the Tokugawa Shogunate issued an edict prohibiting the practice.

This mental training gave the samurai the edge—and the certainty—they needed to act effectively and decisively in difficult situations. It proved to be an invaluable aid not just in combat, but in their roles as leaders and rulers as well.

Musashi clearly responded to this psychological training with exceptional diligence and made use of it in all of his endeavors. His success offers invaluable direction for succeeding at today's challenges.

If you are an athlete, don't neglect to train your mind as well as your body. Make sure your training includes developing the mental discipline necessary for overcoming tough competition. If you are a business executive—or striving to become one—remember that it takes rigorous mental training to develop the focus, energy, and aggressiveness necessary for success.

CHAPTER 8

Clear the Mind

One feature of the samurai's psychological training that Musashi emphasized was developing the Zen-based capability for "clearing the mind"—that is, eliminating the chorus of thoughts and images that constantly swirl in the brain and interfere with the coherent and efficient function of both the brain and the body.

The most common Zen way of clearing the mind is *zazen* (zah-zen), or "seated meditation." There is indisputable evidence, in both practical applications and clinical research, that meditation or "clearing the mind" improves your ability to think more clearly and function more effectively.

However, getting control of the mind is far more difficult to do than you might imagine. One Japanese master, after a lifetime of training in meditation, said that during his entire life he had succeeded in having complete control of his mind for only three seconds.

From the fourteenth century on, all samurai were taught to meditate regularly as a way of strengthening control over their minds and enhancing their sensory perceptions. Musashi obviously mastered the Zen way of meditating, and attributed much of his success in battle and in the arts to this simple practice.

There are many occasions when turning the mind off is the best thing to do. If your body has been sufficiently trained, it can then do what it is supposed to do. In Japanese, this state is known as *mushin* (muu-sheen), or "no mind," as well as *muga* (muu-gah), meaning "no ego." According to Zen Buddhism, once a person is in a state of *mushin/muga*, accomplishing a task is as easy as thinking it.

Musashi tried to totally empty his mind of all distractions—even the various forms and techniques of fighting that he had mastered! He wanted to be absolutely free to use whatever approach, tactic, or technique that came naturally to the situation at hand. His philosophy was that every movement should be absolutely natural to the mind and body so that it can be accomplished without having to plan or think about it. This is, of course, the mark of a champion athlete or a master of any art, including painting, juggling, or using a bow and arrow.

Meditation has long been a cultural custom in Japan, practiced by most people at some time or another, and regularly by priests, tea masters, artists, landscape gardeners, potters, warriors, and businesspeople. Some of modern-day Japan's most successful businessmen meditate to enhance their decision-making and management skills. A few Japanese corporations even require all of their managers to spend time in temples meditating under the strict supervision of Buddhist priests.

A Japanese Olympic diving champion who had been performing under par during the early qualifying performances turned everything around on her last two attempts and came through like the champion she was. When asked how she had done it, she replied: "I turned my mind off and just did what came natural [to my body]."

Most people today are so caught up in the chaos and cacophony of modern life and work that they are unable to use even the smallest percentage of the power of their own minds.

It therefore goes without saying that people would benefit from meditating. But it should especially be a part of the training and the regular routine of all people in leadership or management positions—in business, in politics, and in the military.

This is another area in which a very small change in lifestyle—fifteen to twenty minutes a day of meditating—could have far-reaching effects. If nothing else, it would improve your mental and physical health and contribute to a longer and more tranquil life. If meditation doesn't work for you, develop your own means of "clearing" your mind so that you can focus more lucidly and act more effectively.

CHAPTER 9

The Power of Emptiness

Musashi's mental training went beyond clearing the mind of extraneous thoughts and preconceived notions. His point was that a completely empty mind made it possible for one to respond spontaneously to the circumstances at hand, and gave him a special power over his opponents. In fact, his fighting style was based as much on what he called "the power of emptiness" as on his skill with weapons. A point that he made over and over was the importance of not letting the mind interfere with one's actions—a weakness that most of us are familiar with.

He said this factor was especially important when fighting more than one person at the same time. It was especially vital when facing a large group of fighters who have attacked you and are determined to cut you down. His secret was to completely empty his mind of any second thoughts, any fear, or anything else, and let his body do what he had trained it to do.

Musashi gave *more* credit to the power of emptiness than he did to his ability with the sword—which, as he noted, was something any other well-trained warrior could match. His point was that to do something perfectly, whether in fighting or in painting or any other art, it was necessary to let your well-trained body and your subconscious direct your actions. This Zen Buddhist concept was at the heart of the extraordinary skill of many of Japan's master artists and craftsmen—from painters to garden designers.

Again, this is something that great competitors know instinctively and practice unconsciously. Where business and other affairs are concerned, the point is to know your subject absolutely, practice its execution until it is automatic, and then proceed without any doubts or mental reservations.

CHAPTER 10

Learn from Your Opponents

Musashi developed an incredible ability to really perceive the things he looked at—not just physical objects, but movements and patterns, like those of the sun, animals, birds, water, and people. He studied these until their essence—including how they manifested themselves—became clear to him. He then incorporated what he had learned into his approach to fighting.

In Musashi's descriptions of his encounters, he explains in detail the weaknesses of his opponents and what he learned from them. His remarkable powers of observation made it possible for him to detect the fighting style of his opponents in a matter of seconds and absorb anything from their style that he considered worthwhile. He could then adjust his own style to overwhelm them, usually in a matter of seconds.

It was apparently this ability to observe, learn, and adapt nearly instantly that made it possible for Musashi to become an unbeatable swordsman without having a tutor.

The obvious lesson here: Study your opponents and competitors carefully. Know their strengths and their weaknesses precisely. Learn from them, adapt your approach to take advantage of their weaknesses, and then defeat them before they realize that you have changed your tactics.

CHAPTER 11

Pay Attention to Details

Among the training precepts recorded by the samurai-scholars of the fifteenth and sixteenth centuries, the importance of paying special attention to small details was high on the list. One of the more popular axioms of the samurai reminded them to treat great things casually and small things seriously—as if their life depended on these details, as it often did. In his treatise on his way of fighting, Musashi emphasized that paying attention to small details was one of the most critical aspects of winning any battle, or succeeding in any enterprise.

Musashi made the point that people who fail in large enterprises often do so because they ignore the little things, or leave them to people who are not absolutely dependable. He pointed out that in battles to the death, warriors who did not personally maintain their weapons, who had not studied their own strengths and weaknesses and developed plans to either use them or compensate for them, or who failed to study their opponents carefully were not likely to live long.

Throughout his lifetime, Musashi practiced his philosophy through constant study and training, never assuming that he had learned everything he needed to know, or that the little details would take care of themselves.

Present-day businesspeople who fail may not be in danger of losing their lives, but if they do not understand the details of the business they are in, especially what really makes it work, they are not likely to succeed. Taking Musashi's advice to heart can give you a major advantage.

CHAPTER 12

The Power of Silence

To the average Westerner, silence is the absence of sound, has no form or essence, and performs no function of its own. In the traditional Japanese mind-set, however, silence has both form and an essence, and it plays a vital role in achieving control of the mind, in the creative process and in communicating with nature and with people.

Musashi was a master at using silence as one of his most powerful weapons. He was silent most of his life, in part, perhaps, because he spent so much of his life alone. Not only did he not boast about his accomplishments, when he did talk or write, he played them down and spoke only in the humblest of terms. His thoughts therefore remained unknown to most of the people he met in his lifetime.

This had both positive and negative effects. On the one hand, his silence created an aura of mystery about him that was often an asset. It made some people curious to meet him or afraid to challenge him, which he often used to his advantage. On the other hand, it made many people think he was not altogether right in the head. They would speak disparagingly of him—saying that since he spent so much time traveling, without so much as a change of clothing, he was not fit to be welcomed into any home.

Whatever the case, his manner resulted in people viewing him with strong emotions. Some regarded him as a fool. Others regarded him as someone who did not behave properly and was therefore neither a worthy opponent nor an acceptable guest.

During many of his encounters with men determined to kill him Musashi never spoke, and he often behaved as if they were not there. This lack of any sign of emotion or interest unnerved or puzzled his opponents, giving him an advantage before the first move. He either cut them down before they got their wits together, or he killed them when they forgot to be cautious and rushed in to strike him.

The lesson for businesspeople is clear: While there can be great advantages to sharing information with your business partners, it can also be extremely important not to reveal too much about your assets, your plans, or your intentions in advance—something that present-day Japanese businessmen do automatically.

CHAPTER 13

Change the Rules of Engagement

Adhering precisely to a highly stylized and formal etiquette was (and is) the basis for Japanese morality. During the long reign of the samurai class (1192–1868) failure to conform to the prescribed etiquette was, in effect, a moral and a secular sin that often was punishable by death. There was a precise way of doing everything, from the most mundane actions to the most exalted ceremonies and rituals—including *harakiri* and engaging in duels.

Adherence to a strict, formal etiquette is still the standard of behavior among virtually all adults in Japan, and it continues to distinguish the Japanese from other people. Young Japanese, influenced by the Western concepts of individuality and independence, typically ignore the traditional etiquette when interacting among themselves in personal situations, but in order to be accepted into the adult world, they must conform to the traditional etiquette in speech as well as in their physical behavior. Japan's traditional culture remains so strong in the adult world that it is not likely to disappear any time soon.

One of Musashi's favorite and most effective weapons was the power of unexpected behavior. This was an especially powerful weapon because Japanese standards of behavior were precisely prescribed forms that had been programmed into his opponents from infancy. His adversaries were often so shocked by his unconventional and "non-conforming" behavior that they lost their presence of mind, and their lives.

Musashi was described as a wayward youth who often misbehaved, so he obviously grew up being a maverick as far as the detailed choreography of Japanese etiquette was concerned. He also obviously observed how unexpected (un-Japanese) behavior upset everyone, and he made this knowledge part of his arsenal of tactics in fighting.

For example, Musashi carried and used two swords—a long one and a short one, and called his way of fighting *Niten* (nee-tane), "Two Heavens," or "Two Swords Style." His skill was such, however, that in most of his later fights to the death he used wooden rather than steel swords—something that infuriated his opponents because they regarded such behavior as treating them and the exalted code of the samurai with contempt.

The power of the unexpected was dramatically demonstrated by two of Musashi's most famous duels—one in Kyoto when he was twenty-one, where he killed several well-known warriors over a three-day period, and the another when he met an opponent, by prearrangement, on a beach on a secluded island (known as "Boat Island" because of its silhouette).

On the first day of the Kyoto affair, Musashi showed up late for an appointed duel with the head of a group of some one hundred warriors of a leading clan. His meticulously mannered opponent became furious, losing his cool and then his life. Musashi then arranged to fight the leader's brother, who was second in command of the group, on the following day. He showed up late again, with the same result—he killed the infuriated and overwrought warrior immediately.

On the third day, Musashi was supposed to fight the son of the man he killed the first day. This time he arrived early, taking the over one hundred clan members who had gathered to take revenge by surprise. Jumping out of the early morning mist into the crowd of warriors before they got their wits about them, Musashi instantly cut down his designated opponent and then began herding the group of warriors before him as if they were sheep, killing one after the other until the remainder of the group turned and fled.

In the "Boat Island" duel, which occurred when he was twenty-nine (in 1612), Musashi arrived at the island some two hours late. He had deliberately slept late, eaten a leisurely breakfast, and then carved a wooden sword out of an oar before being rowed out to the island.

His opponent, Kojiro Sasaki, a huge warrior much feared for his prowess with a sword and his reputation for having killed many men in duels, was so furious at Musashi for "breaking the rules" that he rushed toward him, throwing away his scabbard at the same time.

Musashi yelled out, "You have already lost!" He evaded the enraged warrior's slashing sword and struck him on the head with a blow that knocked him to the ground. Sasaki was unconscious but still alive. Musashi struck him a second time, this time on the chest, killing him.

This lesson applies to competition of all kinds—unexpected behavior can disrupt your opponents' most carefully developed plans and give you the opening you need to press your advantage.

CHAPTER 14

The Power of Fear

It goes without saying that fear can be upsetting and debilitating, and can be used to make powerful opponents more vulnerable to attack. Musashi was a master at using fear to weaken his opponents. Sometimes he would remain silent and unmoving, making his opponents anxious about him and his fighting style. Then he would crush them with such speed and violence that he seemed to be possessed by some demon. On other occasions he would suddenly lunge at an opponent and let out a shriek to startle them, making it possible for him to cut them down before they had time to react.

Musashi was so accomplished that, according to eyewitness accounts, he sometimes caught the sword of an opponent between the palms of his bare hands as it descended toward his head—an incredible feat that was one of the reasons why he became so feared, respected, and praised during his lifetime. This tactic of catching an opponent's sword as it descends is a mainstay of some of the heroes of Japan's famous samurai movies, commonly referred to as *chambara* (chahm-bah-rah)—a word that refers to the noise made by clashing swords. The *chambara* films are the Japanese equivalent of American Westerns, with their gunslinger heroes.

Musashi always had an additional edge—his opponents did not know what fighting style he was going to use and therefore had to fear attacks that would leave them defenseless. Moreover, the fact that he had killed a number of famous warriors before he was out of his teens surely added some measure of fear in all of his subsequent opponents. Using fear as a tactic was certainly not something that Musashi originated, but few have used it with more skill and success, especially in one-on-one encounters where one of the combatants was going to die.

Frightening your opponents might not be appropriate for a businessperson—it might even be a great way to lose business—but a certain level of intimidation can be invaluable in negotiations or competition. The lesson here is to take advantage of any reasonable leverage you can bring to a contest. As is well known to many athletes, anything you can do to rattle your opponent gives you the upper hand.

CHAPTER 15

Confuse Your Opponent

Musashi used the power of confusion with deadly efficiency during many of his duels to the death and with the hundreds of men he later fought without intending to kill them. It is obvious that individuals who are suddenly confused or thrown off guard are not in full command of their faculties and can make mistakes that they wouldn't ordinarily make. All Musashi had to do was get an opponent to hesitate for one or two seconds. That was all the time he needed to strike a fatal blow.

One of his fighting tactics was what he called "the rhythm of striking an opponent in one count." This was assuming a pose with his sword that made it appear that he was vulnerable to attack, resulting in the opponent concentrating on the opening. Musashi then cut the opponent down in one quick movement before he had time to draw his sword back.

On other occasions, he lowered his sword as if he had forgotten where he was. Again, his surprised opponent, seeing what he thought was an opening, would spring forward recklessly, only to be met by a move so fast he was unable to dodge or block it.

Of course, confusing and misleading opponents is a classic tactic in virtually any kind of engagement. The less time they have to prepare themselves, the more likely you are to succeed. In military conflicts especially, using false starts, apparent inaction, or dramatic misdirection to tilt the advantage in your favor before the fighting begins can mean the difference between victory and defeat.

CHAPTER 16

The Mind as a Weapon

In his treatise on fighting, Musashi repeatedly said that it was far better to defeat your opponent with your mind than with a weapon—meaning that it was better to first "strike" with the mind to weaken or virtually disarm an opponent and then, if necessary, use your sword to finish the job.

He used a variety of ruses that gave him a major psychological advantage in his fights. These included arriving late for a fight, arriving early for a fight, not using the expected sword, saying nothing at all or saying something that would rattle his opponents, and so on. These were all simple things that he knew would upset his opponents and distract them from the battle at hand.

On one famous occasion, Musashi approached a skilled swordsman with a stick of firewood instead of a sword and killed him with a single blow to the head. It is hard to say, from this distance, exactly why Musashi was able to kill the warrior in a split second with a piece of wood. It may have been because he was so fast and so deadly that his opponent didn't have time to defend himself, or he may have been so rattled by Musashi's unorthodox weapon that he was unable to function.

Musashi obviously understood at a very young age that breaking your opponents' mental concentration was one of the best ways to weaken them. Again, behaving in such a way that his opponents could not anticipate what he was going to do was one of his most successful tactics.

Of course, this kind of psychological warfare has always been a part of war—from shouting and beating on drums to broadcasting loud music and propaganda to dropping leaflets from the air. Modern-day warriors who resort to the force of arms in actual fighting or confrontations may be taking on their opponents the hard way. They should not hesitate to improvise and do the unexpected. They might find that the edge they gain actually reduces the chances of a deadly, destructive conflict.

CHAPTER 17

See What Cannot Be Seen

Japanese movies about the feats of samurai often portray the hero "seeing" things that the average person cannot see, and somehow "knowing" the exact location of an object or enemy that is hidden behind walls or other obstacles. Some of these portrayals are obviously exaggerated, but it is a matter of record that many Zen priests and samurai warriors honed their senses to the point that they could, in fact, see and hear things that were invisible and inaudible to others.

The founder of Zen, the Indian priest Bodhidharma, is said to have reached the point that he could hear the conversations of ants. (He sat before a wall—meditating—for nine years!) It is also said that some warriors could hear the difference between the rustle of silk garments in a distant hallway and fluttering leaves outside a house.

Musashi practiced meditating regularly and made much of being able "to see what cannot be seen" in his instructions to his disciples, so we can assume that he himself had developed his "extrasensory perception" to a high level. Musashi used a Zen Buddhist term meaning "to look through" in his treatise. The term he used also means to understand the essence of what is being looked at. With this understanding, one can react correctly to things or events both near and far.

The point here is not to spend years meditating in order to have superman eyes and ears, but to reach the point where you are always calm, collected, and sensitive to the developments around you. Once you have achieved this level of tranquility and sensitivity, it may seem as if you are "seeing what cannot be seen," and you will have a distinct advantage over competitors who have not developed their senses to the same degree.

CHAPTER 18

Don't Get Stuck on One Style

One of Musashi's primary goals in traveling about the country and meeting other samurai in duels and in demonstration bouts (called "comparisons of technique") was to observe and learn their different styles of fighting. The more familiar he became with the variety of fighting tactics, the less likely he was to see a style he hadn't seen before or didn't know how to defeat.

In his years of observing the behavior of other samurai in training and in his encounters with dozens of them in duels, Musashi discovered that virtually all of them followed a precise form in their combat—from the way they placed and moved their feet to how they held and used their swords. These men, obviously, were conditioned mentally and physically to precisely follow the fighting styles they had been taught. Musashi realized that this was a major weakness that left the warriors vulnerable to opponents who understood their style of fighting and could respond with tactics designed to counter them.

Musashi made it his practice to never depend on any particular form, even those that he had perfected. His approach was to change to any style that would give him an advantage over his opponent.

Whether in battle, business, or sports, people tend to go with what they have been taught and what has worked for them in the past—even if it is not working in the present. The moral, of course, is don't get stuck on any one way of doing things. You are more likely to succeed if you change your tactics the moment it becomes obvious that the old ways are not working.

Musashi's message is simple: Once you have mastered your weapons and tactics, forget about form and do what comes naturally in response to the circumstances at hand.

CHAPTER 19

The Importance
of Flexibility

"Water" was one of the "five rings" making up the foundation of Musashi's fighting strategy and tactics. He chose water because it is one of the most flexible of all things in nature, conforming itself instantly and without effort to whatever shape it encounters. Moreover, water moves in the direction of least resistance without any effort whatsoever, and it eventually overcomes even the most powerful barrier.

Musashi also made a special point of observing that when one's efforts are blocked and progress cannot be made against an opponent, one should imitate water that has been constrained behind a dam that suddenly collapses and rushes forward with incredible speed and power.

He taught that the mind of the samurai should be "like water"—the epitome of flexibility, able to change instantly to conform to and take advantage of any circumstance. Flexibility was, in fact, at the core of virtually everything that Musashi taught. He went further than advising his disciples to "be" flexible in fighting; he said that they should "absorb" flexibility into their minds as well as their bodies so that it came naturally to them without them having to think about it. Only this way, Musashi continued, can one avoid being surprised or caught off guard by anyone or anything.

He added that the frame of mind for one who has mastered flexibility is serenity or tranquility and that one of the key assets of the master swordsman is a tranquil mind. The lessons for people in the modern world are obvious.

CHAPTER 20

Make Sure You See the Big Picture

Musashi realized that everything in nature, including the affairs of men, is in a constant state of flux—that nothing remains the same from one instant to the next. He sometimes compared the human mind with the water in a stream: It looks the same but it is always moving. (As we've seen, Water was one of the five symbols he used in his *Book of Five Rings*.)

In Musashi's philosophy, one was to keep an "open mind." He meant this not just in the general sense of being open to new ideas but in the specific moment-to-moment sense of not letting your mind focus on any one idea, feeling, object, or situation to the point where it distracts you from the events right in front of you.

One of Musashi's most effective tactics was to avoid focusing solely on an opponent's face, body, or weapon, because this prevented him from seeing the whole scene. His goal was to use his eyes like a wide-angle camera lens, allowing him to see everything in the immediate area. He was able to "see" himself, his opponent, and their surroundings as if he were viewing them from outside his own body, from an angle that allowed him to see the whole scene.

Musashi thus became as much a spectator as a participant in his battles. It is well known that spectators can see the weaknesses and mistakes made by fighters (and others) and recognize opportunities far more clearly than the participants themselves.

Another of his tactics was to never "stop the mind"—that is, to never focus on one thing long enough to prevent him from seeing everything else that was going on at the same time. He said that focusing the mind (his actual words were "putting the mind in one place") raised the risk of "falling into one-sidedness."

He maintained that your mind and your vision should be perfectly free to flow as water does, expanding and contracting to meet the circumstances of the moment. This understanding was crucial to Musashi's success as a warrior and his survival into old age.

In today's world, this means not focusing too much on the task at hand. This may sound paradoxical, given Musashi's instructions to pay careful attention to the details, but in fact these are just different ways of making the same point.

Musashi's commonsense suggestion was that we must also pay careful attention to events or situations seemingly in the background or on the periphery if we want to completely understand what is happening around us. Without this attention to the "edges" of situations, we are at risk of being blind-sided by threats or events we do not see coming.

CHAPTER 21

Use Time as a Weapon

The idea that "time is money" developed in Europe following the Industrial Revolution, when financiers began to establish businesses to make a profit and people began to work for wages. But long before that era, linear-thinking Westerners looked at time as something that stretched out before them in more or less a straight line, as something that could be measured in seconds, minutes, hours, days, and that if not used, it was wasted.

The traditional Japanese, by comparison, thought of time as a circle. All things came and went and were not measured by a clock ticking off seconds, minutes, and hours but by the seasons and other natural cycles. Instead of trying to do more things faster, the Japanese were more inclined to slow things down and do them better.

As a result, the Japanese build "space" or "time gaps" into whatever project they are engaged in, especially in business and political negotiations. This allows time for the two sides to rest, to clarify, strengthen, or reaffirm their positions. These time gaps are generally not planned or even acknowledged. They are taken for granted because they are built into the culture.

Since the Japanese see time differently from Westerners, they do not see these time gaps, called *ma* (mah) in Japanese, as "empty." They see them as part of the process of communicating, negotiating, and reaching consensus. Or they may be used as a tactic to table or block a proposal or project.

Musashi also used time as a weapon, but his approach was exactly the opposite of the traditional Japanese way. Instead of slowing things down, as others expected him to, he sped them up. He acted with such speed that he became almost invisible to his opponents, gaining an incomparable advantage.

He was able to capitalize on his opponents' assumptions or expectations about time to catch them off guard. In today's world, such cultural "assumptions" are often very subtle and may be difficult to detect, much less take advantage of. But a thorough knowledge of your opponent's cultural background and expectations can be invaluable in any kind of competition—and especially so in war.

CHAPTER 22

Never Stop Learning

The concept of continuous learning throughout one's lifetime has gained considerable cachet in the United States and elsewhere in recent times. But we are still far behind the Japanese, and it often shows.

The concept of continuous learning came to Japan along with a wide range of arts and crafts that were imported from China and Korea between 400 and 700 AD. These imports were accompanied by the master-apprentice approach to teaching and training. Training in all skills was manual, intellectual, philosophical, and spiritual, and it continued for up to thirty years or more in some of the more demanding arts and crafts. For the Japanese, the practice of learning over a long period of time became an integral part of their lifestyle and a measure of their cultural expectations.

The advent of the samurai period in 1192 gave new impetus to the concept of continuous learning. The samurai had to continue honing their physical and mental combat skills throughout their active years as warriors because their lives depended on it.

By the fifteenth century, the emerging "code of the samurai" required that warriors also become skilled in literature, especially in poetry, and other fine arts. This made it necessary for them to devote years of study to these new disciplines as well as keep up with the martial arts that were the core of their profession and their class.

With the coming of peace in the early decades of the Tokugawa Shogunate (1603–1868), the samurai class's involvement in the arts and crafts became even more important. Eventually it reached the point where knowledge of literature and the arts was regarded as essential to their social and moral standing.

This desire for learning became extraordinarily conspicuous in Japanese society following the fall of the shogunate government in 1868 and the rush to industrialize and modernize the economy. It is no exaggeration to say that the Japanese became obsessed with learning Western technology and Western ways.

This obsession became even stronger during the post-World War II years, when the Japanese were faced with the challenge of rebuilding their cities and their industries. Students studied until they were exhausted and often ruined their health. Japanese businessmen became famous world-wide for collecting and devouring every scrap of technological and business information they could beg, borrow, or steal.

During the 1950s and '60s hundreds of thousands of Japanese businessmen traveled abroad on research missions, visiting factories, retail outlets, and other businesses with cameras in hand and notebooks at the ready. They were samurai in everything except their apparel—and in carrying cameras instead of swords.

By the time Musashi reached the age of twenty-nine he had become undefeatable in battle, which prompted him to stop killing his opponents. He began combining his daily training in martial arts with instruction in the fine arts. He was still "in training" until the last months of his life, when illness robbed him of his strength and the use of his hands.

Musashi had the rare distinction of being relatively long lived for a samurai. He experienced and adapted to dramatic changes in the roles of the samurai in Japanese society. He had taken on all opponents, all challenges, to fulfill his life-long goals. But in keeping with the ethics of his time, he had achieved more than becoming the greatest swordsman in the history of the country. Before the end of his life he had become a renowned calligrapher, a skilled artist, and a noted writer, known as much for his artistic accomplishments as his prowess with the sword.

This kind of successful transformation requires both continuous training and the ability to expand your goals over time. Today this kind of lifespan is taken for granted, and living longer brings with it the need to be just as adaptable and as skillful as Musashi in preserving and building on your skills and success throughout life.

CHAPTER 23

Hit First; Hit Hard!

Musashi had one unfailing rule in his encounters with opponents: Hit first and hit hard. He took this approach in all of the duels that are covered by the historical record and no doubt in all of his other duels as well. He preached this principle to his disciples, and when he set down his rules for succeeding in battle in his *Book of Five Rings*, it was one of the foundations of his way of fighting. He taught his students to:

- Strike before your opponent is ready, while he is still assuming his fighting stance.
- Catch him off guard, then strike with such power that he is shocked.
- Strike to kill, or to crush your opponent completely.

Of course, there is nothing new about this style of fighting. It was probably one of the primary tactics of primitive man tens of thousands of years ago: Get the jump on your enemy or victims and render them helpless or dead before they can protect themselves.

While Musashi was apparently the only samurai who used the "hit-first hit-hard" approach as a key part of his fighting routine, the concept was well known to the shogunate government, fief lords, and clan leaders of his time, and it was common in the civil wars and internal struggles fought throughout Japan's middle ages.

Of course, the best-known recent example of the attack-first-and-hard tactic was the Japanese aerial raid on Pearl Harbor in 1941. The offensive wars launched by the Japanese military on the Asian mainland prior to 1941 also began with all-out surprise attacks. In modern-day Japan, "the hit-first hit-hard" tactic has been integrated into everyday business strategy—with an emphasis on developing new products that are extraordinarily innovative and create large businesses quickly.

The lesson here is clear: If you find yourself in combat or competition, don't give your opponents an opportunity to settle into a strong position. Strike fast and strike hard—before they have a chance to get the upper hand.

CHAPTER 24

Use All of Your Weapons

Musashi's motto was, "Acknowledge the gods, but don't depend on them." He, of course, depended on his own wits, abilities, and actions to succeed in combat, rather than some divine assistance.

In our society, unlimited or uninhibited conflict or competition of any kind is rare—except in "ultimate fighting" exhibitions and in terrorist acts. Academics, sports, business—even wars—are conducted according to rules of "proper behavior"—originally as determined by mutual agreement but now by public opinion polls!

In Musashi's time, however, combat and competition were driven by commonsense evaluation of goals and methods, many of which are not generally acceptable today. Musashi knew that whether or not he was successful in—or even survived—a duel depended on his using every trick, tool, and technique at his disposal. As we have seen, he would often attack opponents before they were ready. He would take advantage of the fact that fighters are vulnerable during and immediately after they attack: tricking his opponents into rushing at him and then cutting them down before they could deliver a blow.

The lesson here is obvious: In deadly conflicts use whatever tactic or technique you need to accomplish your goals. It is not enough to win the public relations battle if in the process you lose the war.

CHAPTER 25

The Samurai and the Carpenter

In his lessons to his disciples, Musashi used the analogy of a carpenter. He said the samurai should think like a carpenter—in the sense of the tools a carpenter uses, how he maintains the tools, how he trains with the tools, how he plans each project, how he accounts for location and environment and all the other factors that may influence the finished product. He noted that a master carpenter must thoroughly understand the nature of the tools he uses, the materials that are the best suited for the purpose, the size and shape of the things he builds, how they are to be used, and so on.

Musashi's point was that learning how to fight and win was not a simple task with only a few elements, but incorporated a whole world of factors and possibilities that took years to master. He said that until the samurai had made himself as carefully shaped and finished as a perfect building or piece of furniture his training was incomplete and he would be vulnerable.

He made a special point of emphasizing that one of the most important skills needed by a master swordsman was insight into the nature of human beings—their strengths, their weaknesses, their spirit, and all of the different attitudes and behaviors commonly found in the makeup of people.

The point here is that individuals should continuously strive to increase their knowledge and improve themselves in a comprehensive, holistic way. Musashi emphasized that success in one field or area contributes to success in other fields—an insight that is often ignored in today's world.

CHAPTER 26

Take the Initiative

Another of the key principles in Musashi's tactics was to always take the initiative in every encounter—to never let your opponent determine the beginning or the progress of a fight. The obvious point to this rule is that by attacking first and seizing and keeping the advantage you can force your opponent to react to your moves rather than you having to react to his.

Musashi notes that you can maintain the initiative even when your opponent makes the first move by reacting faster than his action—taking advantage of his vulnerability during his move. He called this maneuver "stepping on the sword" of your opponent.

He did not, of course, mean literally stepping on your opponent's weapon. He meant executing a move that would counter any move your opponent made, whether it was raising his sword, lowering his sword, shifting his feet, rushing at you, or whatever. This is a secondary measure, however, since one of Musashi's primary rules in a fight is to make the first move, before your opponent has time to get ready.

As long as you are well trained and in the right frame of mind, the advantages of being the first to attack or to counter with an attack that is faster than your opponent's move are obvious in any business or other competitive situation.

CHAPTER 27

Know Your Environment

Musashi made a point of carefully observing the environment around him for everything and anything he could take advantage of in his fights—the time of day; whether it was sunny or cloudy; whether the ground was dry, wet, uneven, rocky, or soft; the presence of rivers, lakes, trees; and so on.

In his *Book of Five Rings*, Musashi described a number of situations in which his immediate surroundings determined his tactics. Whether outside in open fields or indoors in small rooms and hallways, he emphasized the importance of knowing and using the "lay of the land" to your advantage.

While this is clearly relevant to outdoor sports competitions, its application in the business world may not be as obvious. However, any experienced executive will tell you that paying careful attention to room layout, seating arrangements, speaking order, attendees, and so forth—in other words, the geography of the meeting—is of critical importance in succeeding at business negotiations. This is especially true in Japan, where the format and routine of business meetings has been institutionalized and ritualized for centuries.

CHAPTER 28

Watch for a Collapse

Musashi was keenly aware that in time all things collapse—some things over eons of time and other things in a matter of a split second. He used the word "collapse" in reference to the conduct of an army in combat as well as the condition of an individual opponent. He meant that the soldiers or the individual combatants lost their focus and rhythm, making them vulnerable to a swift, coordinated attack.

Musashi cautioned his disciples that they should train themselves to the point that they could instantly recognize when an opponent lost his rhythm and instantly spring to the attack before they could recover. In his words, "Your rushing attack must be instantaneous and strong, and you must cut him down with such vigor that he cannot recover." He further warned his disciples that they should thoroughly understand what he meant by "cutting down with vigor."

This advice is, of course, applicable in business, politics, sports, and war.

CHAPTER 29

Become Your Opponent

The ancient Chinese military sage Sun Tzu taught that one of the primary principles of victory in war was to know your enemy. Musashi's version of this precept was to figuratively "become your opponent"—to get "inside" your opponent's head to the point that you could think like him and thus anticipate any move he might make and strike first.

Musashi described the warrior who could think "only in his own head" as a pheasant holed up in a house, while the man who was going to cut him down was described as a hawk. Musashi said that if you demonstrate the ability to "read your opponent's mind" he will be so intimidated that he will become fearful, make mistakes, and give you an opportunity to defeat him.

He added that if you cannot "see inside of your opponent's head" you should pretend that you do and make a move indicating that you are going to launch an immediate attack. This results in your opponent showing his hand, allowing you to instantly change the nature of your attack, and catch him unprepared. He refers to this ploy as "moving the shadow."

This lesson, too, is applicable in any competitive situation, and particularly so in sports, business, and war.

CHAPTER 30

Draw Your Opponent In

One of the most common tactics Musashi used to give himself an advantage over his opponents was to behave in a casual or lackadaisical manner, resulting in the opponent becoming less watchful and more careless—a move he called "drawing your opponent in." This tactic is, of course, well known, especially to boxers, who employ it to mount swift attacks on their opponents, scoring points and sometimes ending contests with one or two blows.

In a somewhat humorous note, Musashi likened this strategy to getting your opponents drunk. He also related this tactic to acting so unthreatening that your opponent becomes bored, lowers his defenses, and is more susceptible to being crushed by a lightning strike.

The tactic of "drawing an opponent in" has long been an integral part of Japanese culture—not in the manner suggested by Musashi, but as a result of a built-in "humble mode" that historically has resulted in adversaries and competitors underestimating the abilities, strength, and spirit of the Japanese. The samurai culture that endured from the twelfth to the nineteenth century in Japan made it mandatory that common people—and the samurai themselves when interacting with their own superiors—behave in a humble way to avoid giving offense and to maintain a façade of harmony.

This cultural behavior is still very much alive in contemporary Japan and continues to give the Japanese a special advantage in their dealings with others. A significant part of this advantage is the reaction of typical Westerners when they encounter people who are less experienced, less skilled than they are. These Westerners, Americans in particular, instantly go into a "help mode" and go out of their way to help those they perceive as less capable.

The Japanese have long been aware of the "help syndrome" that drives Westerners, and they naturally take advantage of it. In any event, it goes without saying that humility will get you much further than arrogance and braggadocio, and this is something that Musashi thoroughly understood and used with extraordinary success.

CHAPTER 31

Never Use the Same Tactic Twice

Another of Musashi's rules of combat was never to use the same tactic more than twice—and never more than once if you could help it. His obvious intent was to prevent any of his opponents from becoming familiar enough with his style of fighting that they could prepare themselves to counter it.

Conventional wisdom encourages us to develop, or "engineer," specific methods or processes for doing things—

and then repeat them over and over again. This is especially true in situations involving teams and groups and is even more of a factor in large organizations such as corporations, government ministries, and armies. The rationale, of course, is that to achieve shared goals, groups must work in unison in a consistent way. Musashi, of course, would not have agreed. He would have pointed out the danger in consistent and predictable behavior—whether in a duel to the death or competing in tough world markets.

In the past, Japanese culture was the epitome of the organized, prescribed way of doing things. But this started to change during the 1990s as the famous "bubble economy" began to deflate. In desperate efforts to revitalize the economy, Japanese companies turned their most innovative employees loose, letting them work outside of the highly structured company system. They not only separated them from the hierarchical corporate structures, they arranged for separate financing.

The results were extraordinary. Virtually all of the new "side enterprises" flourished, with many of them playing major roles in returning their parent companies to profitability.

This lesson has not been lost on the Japanese, and it is an invaluable lesson for people, companies, and organizations everywhere. You must learn to adapt and change if you want to survive. If you want to be a winner, like Musashi, you must constantly develop new ways of competing, new techniques for overcoming the challenges you face.

CHAPTER 32

Make Your Opponent Change His Style of Fighting

Another secret of Musashi's incredible success in armed combat was his ability to force his opponents to change their style of fighting. Musashi could read the slightest movement of an opponent's sword, feet, eyes, or hands; recognize their intentions; and adjust his fighting style accordingly. His broad knowledge of the martial arts and his ability to switch to a ·more effective style at will gave him an unbeatable advantage.

If his opponents couldn't react and adapt their own fighting approach—especially if they knew only one style of fighting—he would launch an attack against which they had no defense. In most cases his fights were over in seconds. If, on the other hand, an opponent was experienced enough to shift to another style, Musashi would keep the advantage by forcing them to change again and again until they tried a technique they weren't so good at. Then he would cut them down in a flash.

Musashi's experience, adaptability, and reputation gave him an important psychological advantage over his opponents. They knew that even if they could come up with an effective defense for one of his styles of fighting, Musashi would just switch to another style.

Again, this is a testament to the tactical values of unpredictability, the importance of broad knowledge of fighting techniques, the willingness to take the initiative in competition, and the cleverness to stay one step ahead of your opponents. In terms of contemporary competition, it also speaks to the need for broad tactical flexibility and the willingness to change the terms of the competition.

CHAPTER 33

Behave As If You Were Already Dead

As noted by Inazo Nitobe in *Bushido: The Soul of Japan*, the bedrock of the samurai code was personal honor. To a samurai, the fear of being shamed, of being disgraced, was greater than the love of life. Often, a simple slip in upholding one's honor or the honor of one's family could be resolved only by suicide.

One of the primary principles of the education of a samurai was for them to achieve the state of mind in which they regarded themselves as already dead—a mind-set that left them with no fears for their life, no second-guessing of their abilities, and no reason for avoiding life-threatening situations.

Musashi had apparently already absorbed this lesson by the time he was thirteen, when he challenged and killed a veteran swordsman—or he had such incredible confidence in his ability at that young age that he was absolutely certain that he would win and was therefore fearless. Later in life Musashi instructed his own disciples in the principle of behaving as if they were already dead, so it can surely be assumed that this mind-set also played a vitally important role in his own survival and success.

According to Yamamoto Tsunetomo (in *Hagakure: The Book of the Samurai*, translated by William Scott Wilson), "When on the battlefield, if you try not to let others take the lead and have the solid intention of breaking into the enemy lines, then you will not fall behind others. Your mind will become fierce, and you will manifest martial valor. Furthermore, if you are slain in battle, you should resolve to have your corpse facing the enemy."

The lesson to be learned from this samurai code is that one must be prepared to go all the way in achieving great goals. The modern-day equivalent of this attitude is demonstrated in many ways in business, fighting, gambling, and in sports, when individuals and groups take high risks in pursuit of goals.

CHAPTER 34

Avoid Stalemates

Musashi emphasized the importance of avoiding stalemates at all costs, regarding them as failures. He noted that stalemates occur most often when people attempt impractical ventures that they should have avoided in the first place. The worst such stalemates happen during wars, as has been graphically and horribly demonstrated throughout history—from the Trojan War to Korea and Vietnam.

Musashi's approach to combat—constantly changing his style or forcing his opponents to change theirs, confusing and rattling his opponents, and so on—was also designed to avoid stalemates and win. Nevertheless, a few of his demonstration or "comparison of technique" fights ended in draws—with neither side able to gain an advantage. It is probably safe to assume, however, that given Musashi's track record he would have found a way to achieve a decisive victory if the fights had been to the death.

The lesson here is obvious. You should always prepare backup plans that you can turn to quickly if you're faced with a stalemate. In fact, you should have a number of backup plans ready so that you can break any kind of deadlock. Even the smallest advantage generated by changing your approach or introducing some other element can break a stalemate and make a complete victory possible.

CHAPTER 35

Never Give Your Opponent a Second Chance

Another of Musashi's rules was to make sure that his opponents couldn't make a comeback. At least in his earlier years, he didn't believe in defeating or incapacitating his opponents and then withdrawing from the battle. His policy was to kill them.

Musashi believed that you should take the initiative in everything at all times, never letting your opponent rest or regroup—literally never letting an opponent have time to think. He was also adamant about taking advantage of an enemy at the first sign of what he called their "collapse"—meaning any sign of uncoordinated behavior.

This, he said, provided an opening to rush in with great force and crush the opponent. This may seem savage, but it was the reality of Musashi's times. There is also a lesson here that applies to modern-day combat and competition: Don't stop short of neutralizing your opponent's ability to retaliate.

Most people avoid conflict—at work, in competition, or at home. There is a natural tendency to withdraw, compromise, or relent. The lesson we can learn from Musashi is that when the stakes are high (in his case, life or death) you cannot afford to give your opponent an opportunity to recover and possibly turn defeat into victory or simply prolong the fighting and make the outcome uncertain. His message: Don't stop until your victory is complete, total and final.

This lesson was typically applied on a national scale throughout Japan's early history. One famous example: In 1588 Hideyoshi Toyotomi, a reigning warlord during Japan's shogunate era, issued an edict that required all non-samurai to turn in all swords, spears, guns, and any other weapons they had to local officials. The edict made it a major offense for anyone other than the ruling samurai class to have weapons.

As planned, Hideyoshi's edict made it impossible for the common people of Japan to take any kind of mass military action against the samurai class and the government. His policy, continued by his successors, eventually led to several generations of peace for the Japanese and dramatically reduced the incidence of murder and other crimes of violence—helping to make Japan one of the safest societies on earth.

CHAPTER 36

Pierce the Bottom

Musashi repeated himself endlessly in his efforts to help his disciples become master swordsmen. He called one of his key lessons "piercing the bottom"—a euphemistic way of referring to the spirit of adversaries, and something he emphasized in different ways in virtually all of his instructions.

In Musashi's view there were two facets to victory. First, the opponent or opponents should be killed as quickly and as expeditiously as possible. And second, if any opponents were left alive, their spirit should be totally destroyed so that they would never again present a threat.

Musashi called the destruction of the spirit of an enemy "piercing the bottom"—meaning that the mind of the opponent is "pierced" as if with a spear or sword and therefore is "dead." He warned again and again that you should not stop your attack just because your enemy slacks off and/or retreats, because this does not mean that their "bottom has been pierced"—that there is no more hostility, no more ambition, in their hearts. He instructed his disciples to redouble their efforts when an enemy appeared to be losing, quickly "adjusting" their own minds to continue the attack until they were absolutely certain that the spirit of the enemy had been crushed.

This harsh-sounding advice may not be considered appropriate for most nonviolent situations today, but its power cannot be denied.

CHAPTER 37

The Importance of Art in Life

Musashi was in his late twenties before he realized that being the greatest swordsman in the land was not enough—that in order to be fulfilled as a human being it was essential that he become skilled in other areas as well. He then took up the study of several of the arts and crafts of the day, approaching each of them with the same focus and dedication that had made him master of the sword. Within a few years he was acclaimed for his poetry, drawings, sculptures, and pottery, and thereafter he took more pride in these accomplishments than in his ability with a sword.

The importance of art in human life is taken for granted today, but it is too often forgotten after one finishes elementary school. Thereafter its practice plays little or no role in the life of the average person.

Another lesson that can be learned from Musashi is that training and practicing in a number of arts should continue throughout one's life. One of Musashi's most repeated instructions to his disciples was: "Touch upon all of the arts. Develop a discerning eye in all matters." This idea is still reflected today in Japanese culture.

CHAPTER 38

The Sword of the Spirit

Physical skills and knowledge may be worthless if you don't have a strong spirit—in the sense of courage, determination, will power, and vigor. This may not seem like an original concept, but it is a vital one when the stakes are high and you could lose your life or everything you have dreamed about and worked for in an instant.

It was Musashi's belief that a strong spirit was as important as the weapon you used in fighting. He referred to his approach as "the sword of the spirit," meaning that when wielded properly, spirit could be as formidable as a cutting blade. (In the early years of World War II the Japanese believed that their samurai spirit would make it possible for them to defeat the much larger and more powerful United States.)

Musashi's extraordinary spirit was, in fact, one of his most important weapons. Without an indomitable spirit, it's unlikely he would have rushed in to attack a seasoned warrior—known and feared as a master swordsman—in his first duel. He demonstrated the same spirit in all of his hundreds of encounters with opponents throughout his relatively long life. He was still intimidating powerful warriors half his age when he was in his fifties.

Military commanders, corporate executives, and competitors at all levels should obviously cultivate their own fighting spirit. They should also make a great effort to build and sustain the spirits of the men and women who make up their organizations. People who do not understand and promote the importance of spirit should not be in charge of anybody.

It goes without saying that a small number of fighters or workers who are endowed with an indomitable spirit can achieve extraordinary success against much larger forces. In Musashi's words, one such man can defeat ten men; ten such men can beat one hundred, and so on into the thousands. This advice is extremely—and obviously—relevant if you are part of a small company or organization facing much larger competitors. A strong spirit is absolutely essential if you are going to succeed.

CHAPTER 39

Focus on Winning

One of the most important elements in Musashi's philosophy was what he called a "winning attitude." By this he meant that the mind should be totally focused on winning when one was engaged in battle.

In his own battles he made every effort possible to rid his mind of fears, doubts, or reservations of any kind that might distract him. Every fiber of his being, both his mind and his body, was focused on one goal: to win quickly and absolutely.

He stressed that warriors should not neglect their weapons or go into battle expecting to die. In his words, a warrior should always go into combat prepared for—and expecting—victory. And yet, he noted that there were occasions when forfeiting one's life in a hopeless battle was the right thing to do.

This focus on victory at all costs is captured by Yamamoto Tsunetomo in *Hagakure*: "No matter if the enemy has thousands of men, there is fulfillment in simply standing them off and being determined to cut them down, starting from one end. You will finish the greater part of it."

The ability to single-mindedly focus on winning is, of course, a common trait of great champions in sports and other endeavors. But it usually does not apply to people going about their day-to-day affairs—they have not disciplined their minds or bodies to that degree.

We could all benefit from some samurai-like training in perseverance, purpose, and this kind of positive thinking.

CHAPTER 40

The Head of a Rat,
the Neck of a Bull

One of the core concepts of the samurai code, which was passed on to Japan's modern military forces as well as the Japanese in general, was that in any kind of competition when you do not seem to be making progress you should keep foremost in your thoughts "the head of a rat and the neck of a bull." This saying is a reference to the cleverness of the rat and the courage, stamina, and persistence of a bull.

Musashi's manual on his way of fighting emphasized the importance of this concept in individual duels, in military combat on any scale, and in any challenge or task undertaken by ordinary people. Here again, we see that the foundation of Musashi's approach to fighting and winning was based on common sense raised to a high level. Despite couching the details of his strategy and tactics in esoteric and philosophical terms, they were, in fact, pragmatic and practical to the core.

And just as obviously, the cleverness of the rat and the courage and persistence of the bull are characteristics that everyone should seek to develop.

CHAPTER 41

Surpass Today What You Were Yesterday

The one core message in all of the teaching of Musashi for achieving mastery in swordsmanship and other endeavors is that your focus and dedication must be ongoing and never wane. He expressed this principle by saying "you must surpass today what you were yesterday."

This concept is another of Musashi's lessons that became an integral part of Japanese culture, permeating it from top to bottom. The saying is still commonly used by writers, speakers, instructors, and teachers. And it is at the heart of the Japanese concept expressed in the now well-known word *kaizen* (kigh-zen), which translates as "continuous improvement."

There is a tendency in other cultures for most people to stop training, to stop trying to improve, after they reach a certain level of skill—and this is one of the reasons why the Japanese have had an advantage in virtually everything they do. They have been culturally conditioned to never stop training.

It goes without saying that introducing the concept of striving each day to surpass the you of yesterday into education systems around the world could have a remarkable effect in helping to raise the skill levels of people in general. This phenomenon would in turn contribute across the board to the quality of life.

People in all areas of life should take this lesson to heart.

CHAPTER 42

Perseverance and Diligence

It's obvious that to succeed in any difficult and serious undertaking one must persevere—that is, persist in and remain constant to a purpose, an idea, or a task in the face of obstacles and disappointments. And yet, the value and benefits accruing from perseverance are not deeply ingrained in the minds of many people.

The concept of perseverance was one of the foundations

of the samurai culture and was epitomized by the mind-set and behavior of Musashi. He established a goal and never wavered in his pursuit of it. This trait, a part of the training of all samurai, became characteristic of all Japanese as the generations passed—and it is one of the main contributing factors in what the Japanese have achieved since 1945. Perseverance remains a key element in the acculturation of the Japanese and is still conspicuously visible in the character of the majority.

Another trait that has distinguished the Japanese for generations is diligence in every thing they do—diligence that made them capable of achieving extraordinary things; particularly in business and in war. Between 1870 and 1890, the Japanese transformed their country from a handicraft and agricultural base into a fully industrialized economy. Between 1945 and 1970, they not only rebuilt Japan following the devastation of World War II, they turned the country into the world's second largest economy.

The Japanese owe much if not all of this characteristic diligence to the influence of the samurai, whose lives were founded on a code of diligence taught to them from childhood. It was not an esoteric concept that was studied and forgotten. It was a way of life. This influence gradually permeated the common culture.

Musashi was a paragon of extreme diligence. Using Japanese phraseology that is common today, he was a "God of Diligence." He personified this attribute in his own behavior, and taught his disciples that it was absolutely essential for achieving goals befitting a samurai.

CONCLUSION

The Renewal of the
Samurai Spirit

Until the last decades of the twentieth century, virtually all Japanese were trained with samurai-like intensity in their work, in their sports, and in their cultural pursuits—the results of which have been dramatically demonstrated to the world. Modern-day Japanese culture has been diluted to the point that this kind of training in childhood and during the teen years is no longer typical. What the effects of this will be in the future are unclear, but they surely will not be positive.

However, the samurai spirit gained a new lease on life as a result of the collapse of Japan's so-called "economic bubble" in the early 1990s. The shock was felt throughout the country, resulting in corporate leaders, educators, and government leaders calling on a return to the samurai-like discipline and diligence that had once been taken for granted.

All of these calls for a renewal of the samurai spirit, combined with the reality of the shame and disappointment felt by the Japanese, resulted in a boom in the sales of books on the samurai code, and the proliferation of *dojo* teaching *Kendo* (Ken-doh), "The Way of the Sword." If this "transfusion" of the samurai spirit continues long enough, it will help keep Japan a major player in the global economy.

Of course all people everywhere are aware of the benefits of intensive training, but there are still lessons to be learned from the samurai approach of beginning such training in early childhood and continuing it throughout life.

—OWARI—